MW01201276

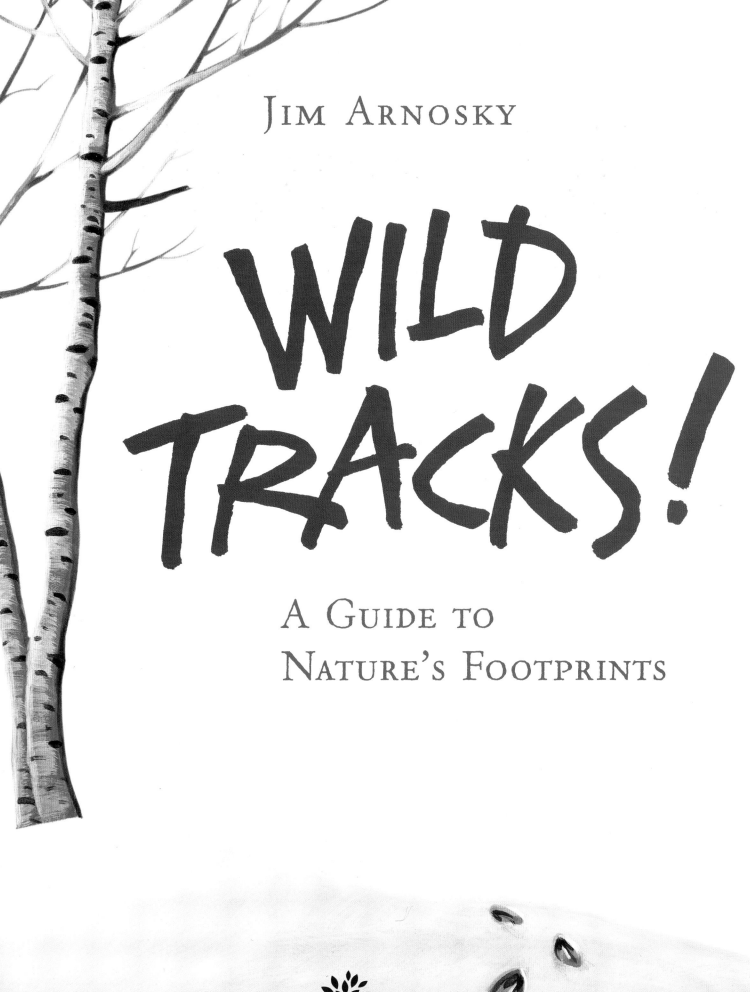

JIM ARNOSKY

WILD TRACKS!

A GUIDE TO
NATURE'S FOOTPRINTS

STERLING
New York / London

This book is for ANNIE in Idaho

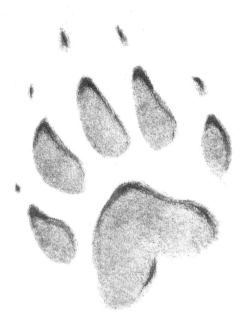

STERLING and the distinctive Sterling logo
are registered trademarks of Sterling Publishing Co., Inc.

LIBRARY OF CONGRESS CATALOGING-IN-PUBLICATION DATA
Arnosky, Jim.
 Wild tracks! : a guide to nature's footprints / Jim Arnosky.
    p. cm.
 ISBN-13: 978-1-4027-3985-9
 ISBN-10: 1-4027-3985-0
1. Animal tracks--Juvenile literature. I. Title.
QL768.A77 2008
591.47'9--dc22
                                                        2007033972

10 9 8 7 6 5 4 3 2 1

Published by Sterling Publishing Co., Inc.
387 Park Avenue South, New York, NY 10016
© 2008 by Jim Arnosky

Distributed in Canada by Sterling Publishing
c/o Canadian Manda Group, 165 Dufferin Street
Toronto, Ontario, Canada M6K 3H6
Distributed in the United Kingdom by GMC Distribution Services
Castle Place, 166 High Street, Lewes, East Sussex, England BN7 1XU
Distributed in Australia by Capricorn Link (Australia) Pty. Ltd.
P.O. Box 704, Windsor, NSW 2756, Australia

The artwork for this book was prepared using pencil and acrylic paints.
Display lettering created by Kirsten Horel
Designed by Lauren Rille

PRINTED IN CHINA.
ALL RIGHTS RESERVED.

Sterling ISBN-13: 978-1-4027-3985-9
       ISBN-10: 1-4027-3985-0

For information about custom editions, special sales, premium and corporate purchases,
please contact Sterling Special Sales Department at 800-805-5489 or specialsales@sterlingpublishing.com.

Contents

ANHINGA

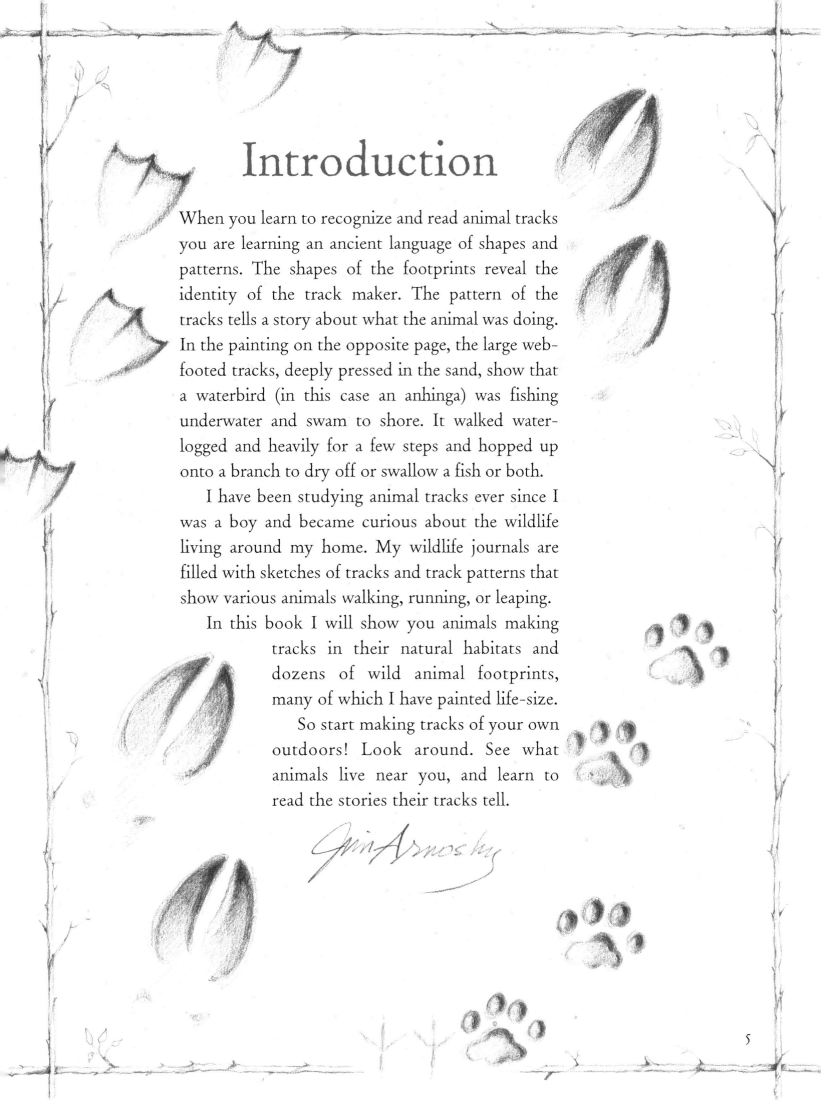

Introduction

When you learn to recognize and read animal tracks you are learning an ancient language of shapes and patterns. The shapes of the footprints reveal the identity of the track maker. The pattern of the tracks tells a story about what the animal was doing. In the painting on the opposite page, the large web-footed tracks, deeply pressed in the sand, show that a waterbird (in this case an anhinga) was fishing underwater and swam to shore. It walked water-logged and heavily for a few steps and hopped up onto a branch to dry off or swallow a fish or both.

I have been studying animal tracks ever since I was a boy and became curious about the wildlife living around my home. My wildlife journals are filled with sketches of tracks and track patterns that show various animals walking, running, or leaping.

In this book I will show you animals making tracks in their natural habitats and dozens of wild animal footprints, many of which I have painted life-size.

So start making tracks of your own outdoors! Look around. See what animals live near you, and learn to read the stories their tracks tell.

Jim Arnosky

WHITE-TAILED DEER

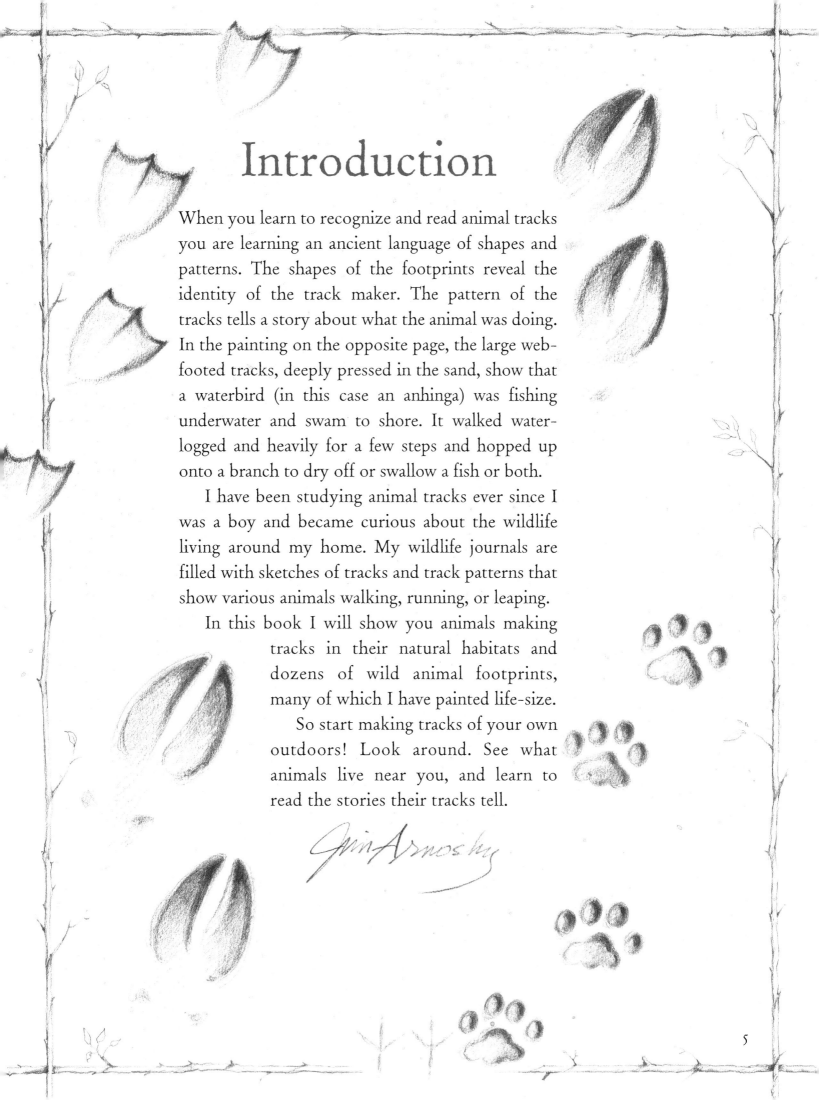

Introduction

When you learn to recognize and read animal tracks you are learning an ancient language of shapes and patterns. The shapes of the footprints reveal the identity of the track maker. The pattern of the tracks tells a story about what the animal was doing. In the painting on the opposite page, the large web-footed tracks, deeply pressed in the sand, show that a waterbird (in this case an anhinga) was fishing underwater and swam to shore. It walked water-logged and heavily for a few steps and hopped up onto a branch to dry off or swallow a fish or both.

I have been studying animal tracks ever since I was a boy and became curious about the wildlife living around my home. My wildlife journals are filled with sketches of tracks and track patterns that show various animals walking, running, or leaping.

In this book I will show you animals making tracks in their natural habitats and dozens of wild animal footprints, many of which I have painted life-size.

So start making tracks of your own outdoors! Look around. See what animals live near you, and learn to read the stories their tracks tell.

Jim Arnosky

WHITE-TAILED DEER

AMERICAN BUFFALO

LIFE-SIZE TRACKS
OF THE DEER FAMILY

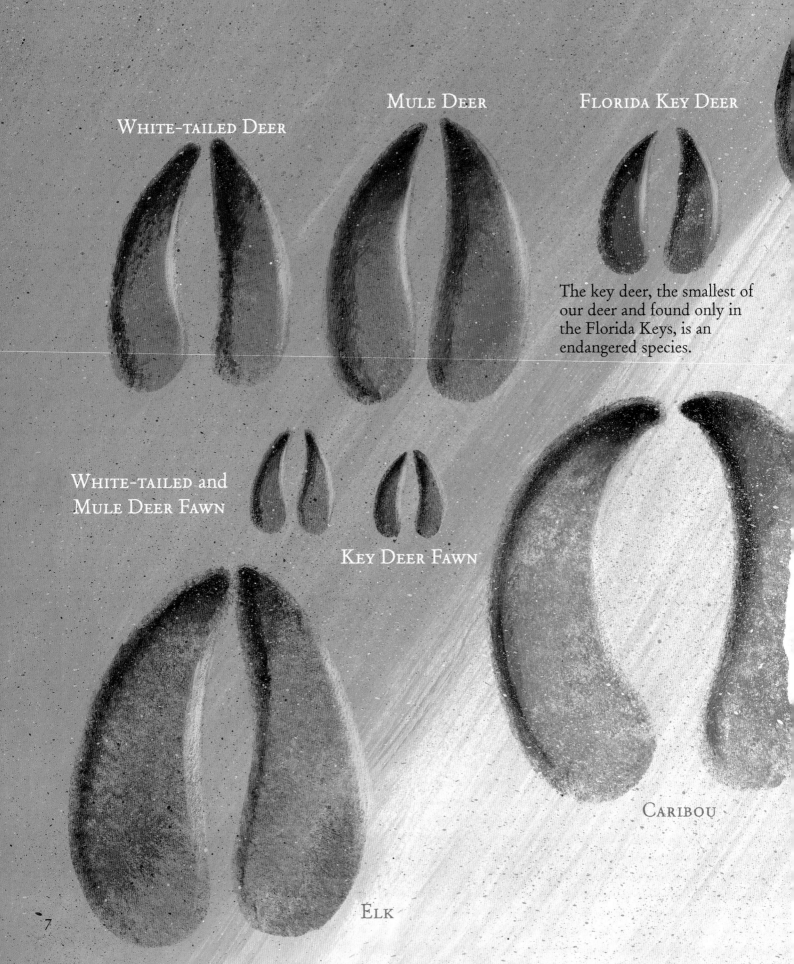

WHITE-TAILED DEER

MULE DEER

FLORIDA KEY DEER

The key deer, the smallest of our deer and found only in the Florida Keys, is an endangered species.

WHITE-TAILED and MULE DEER FAWN

KEY DEER FAWN

CARIBOU

ELK

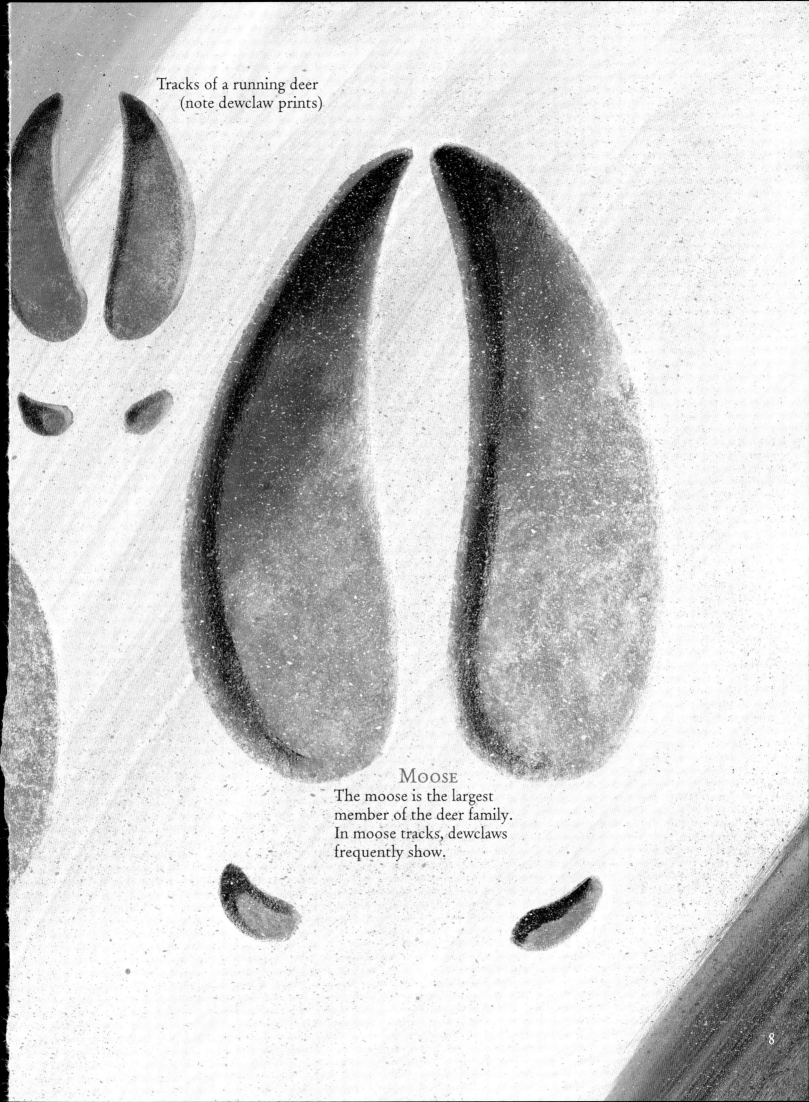

Tracks of a running deer
(note dewclaw prints)

MOOSE
The moose is the largest
member of the deer family.
In moose tracks, dewclaws
frequently show.

8

Deer Tracks

The heart-shaped hoofprints of deer are the most recognizable of all animal tracks. Male deer tend to drag their feet as they walk. The bigger the buck, the deeper the drag marks.

When deer run, their sharp hoofs cut deeply into the ground and their small back toes, called dewclaws, can often be seen in their tracks. Deer running or walking on slippery mud or ice spread their hoofs wide for stability, making their hoofprints look like a set of horns. Reverse hoofprints indicate the deer made an abrupt turnabout to run away.

In autumn—the deer's breeding season—look for fresh marks on small trees where bark has been worn away. These "buck rubs" are made by the antlers of male deer while they are practicing to fight with other males.

The white-tailed deer, shown on the left, is typical of the North American deer family, which also includes elk, caribou, and moose.

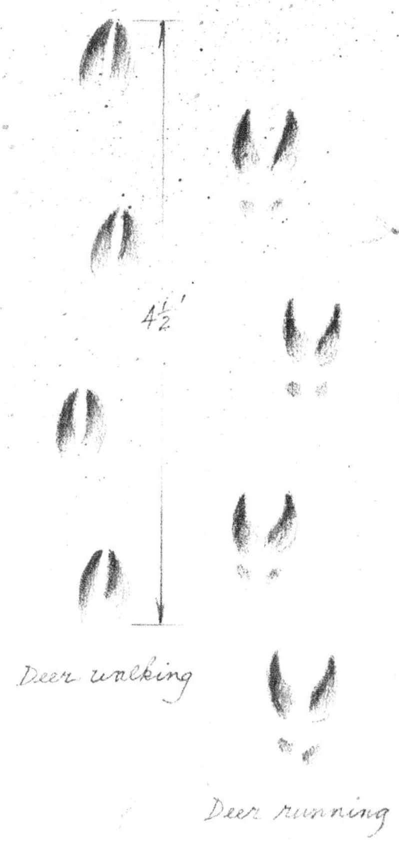

Buck drags in light snow

An abrupt turnabout

4½'

Deer walking

Deer running

Buck rubs

Bottom of a deer hoof

Toenails

Toes

Dewclaw

Top of a deer hoof

BLACK BEAR

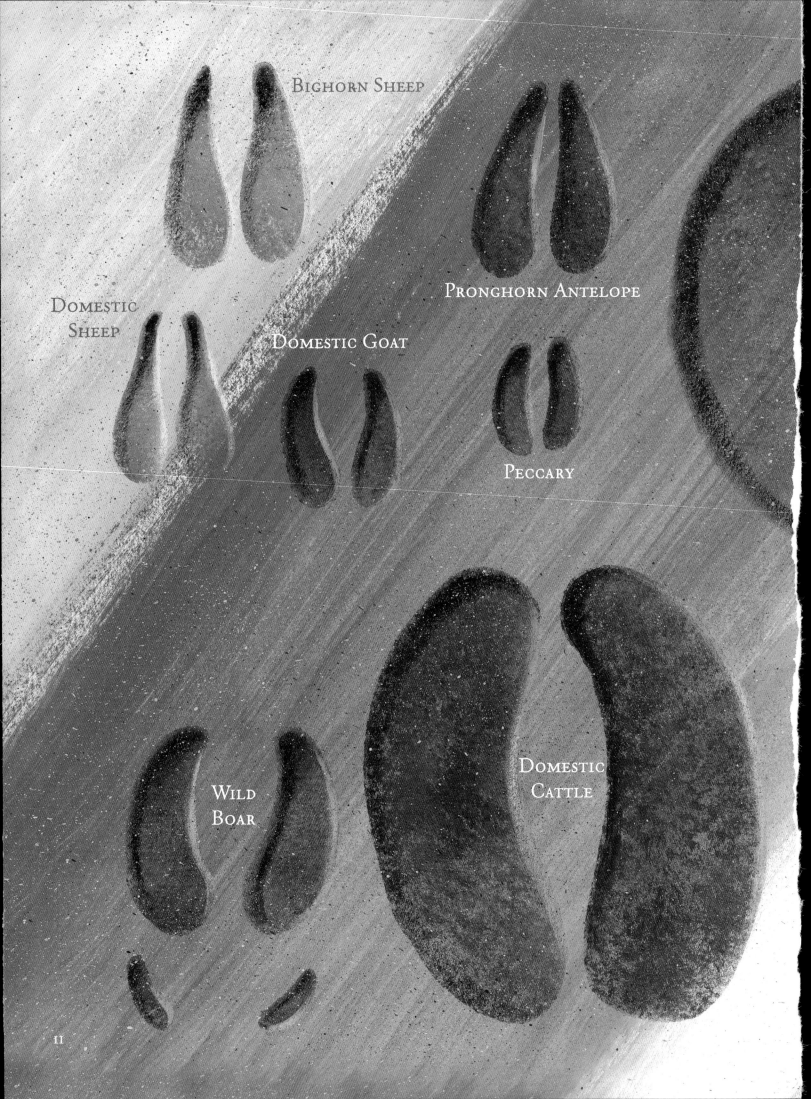

BIGHORN SHEEP

PRONGHORN ANTELOPE

DOMESTIC
SHEEP

DOMESTIC GOAT

PECCARY

WILD
BOAR

DOMESTIC
CATTLE

BUFFALO
The buffalo, or bison, is the largest of all land animals in North America. A bull buffalo can weigh 3,000 pounds and stand 6 feet tall at the shoulder.

BURRO

DOMESTIC PIG

HORSE
(with horseshoe)

LIFE-SIZE TRACKS OF OTHER HOOFED ANIMALS

12

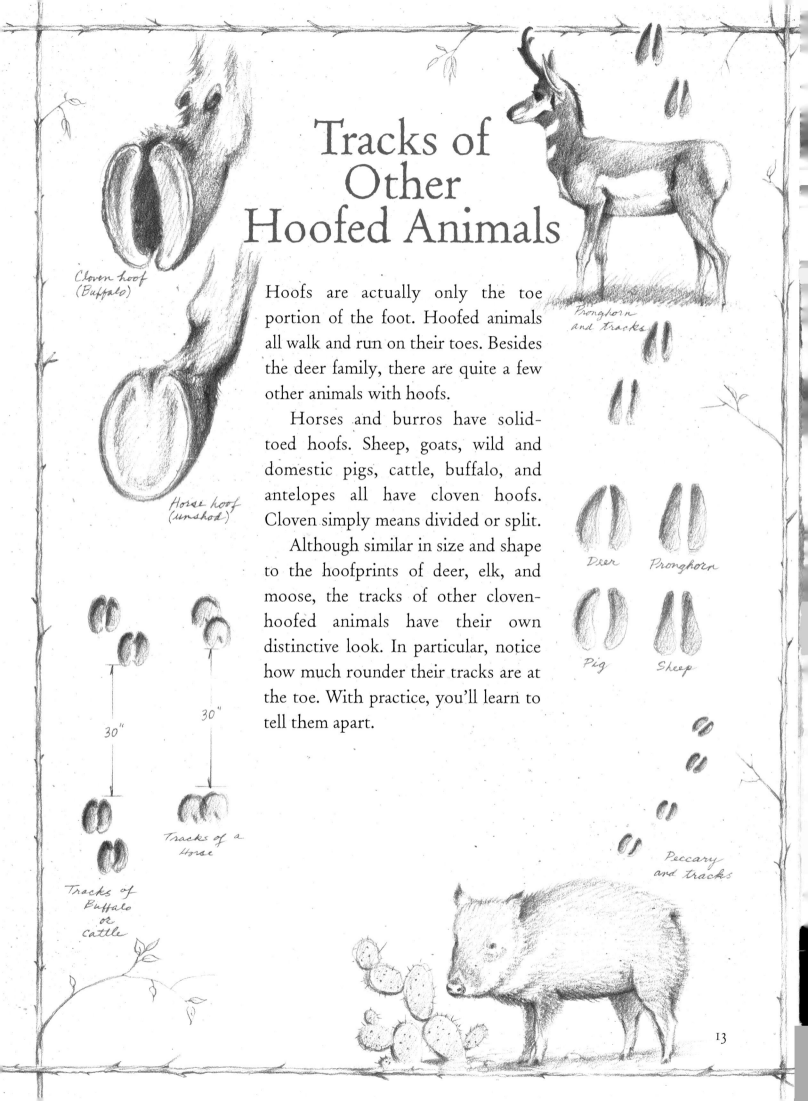

Tracks of Other Hoofed Animals

Cloven hoof
(Buffalo)

Horse hoof
(unshod)

Hoofs are actually only the toe portion of the foot. Hoofed animals all walk and run on their toes. Besides the deer family, there are quite a few other animals with hoofs.

Horses and burros have solid-toed hoofs. Sheep, goats, wild and domestic pigs, cattle, buffalo, and antelopes all have cloven hoofs. Cloven simply means divided or split.

Although similar in size and shape to the hoofprints of deer, elk, and moose, the tracks of other cloven-hoofed animals have their own distinctive look. In particular, notice how much rounder their tracks are at the toe. With practice, you'll learn to tell them apart.

Pronghorn
and tracks

Deer   Pronghorn

Pig   Sheep

30"   30"

Tracks of a
Horse

Tracks of
Buffalo
or
Cattle

Peccary
and tracks

13

Bear Tracks

Bears walk flatfooted, placing the entire foot on the ground with each step. The wide front feet and the large hind feet show completely in bear tracks. When running, the front feet and the front portion of the hind feet show up in the tracks. Because a bear is a heavy animal, its tracks are often pressed deeply, creating perfectly defined footprints. With a perfect set of four bear footprints (two front and two hind), an experienced animal tracker is able to accurately estimate the size and weight of the bear that made them.

On slippery surfaces, a bear's toes spread apart for better traction, pressing in footprints that are much larger than the bear's feet. Such splayed footprints can fool a tracker into imagining the bear that left them is much larger than its actual size.

Black Bear tracks in soft ground

A splayed Track

Running fast

Black Bear claw marks on tree

A Track pattern of a Black Bear running slowly

Black Bear claw (actual size)

Bottom of a Black Bear's hind foot

Bottom of a Black Bear's front foot

LIFE-SIZE TRACKS
OF BEARS

BLACK BEAR
The black bear is found through-
out North America. It is the
smallest of the North American
bears, which include the grizzly,
brown, and polar bears.

**GRIZZLY BEAR and
BROWN BEAR**
(note marks of long claws)

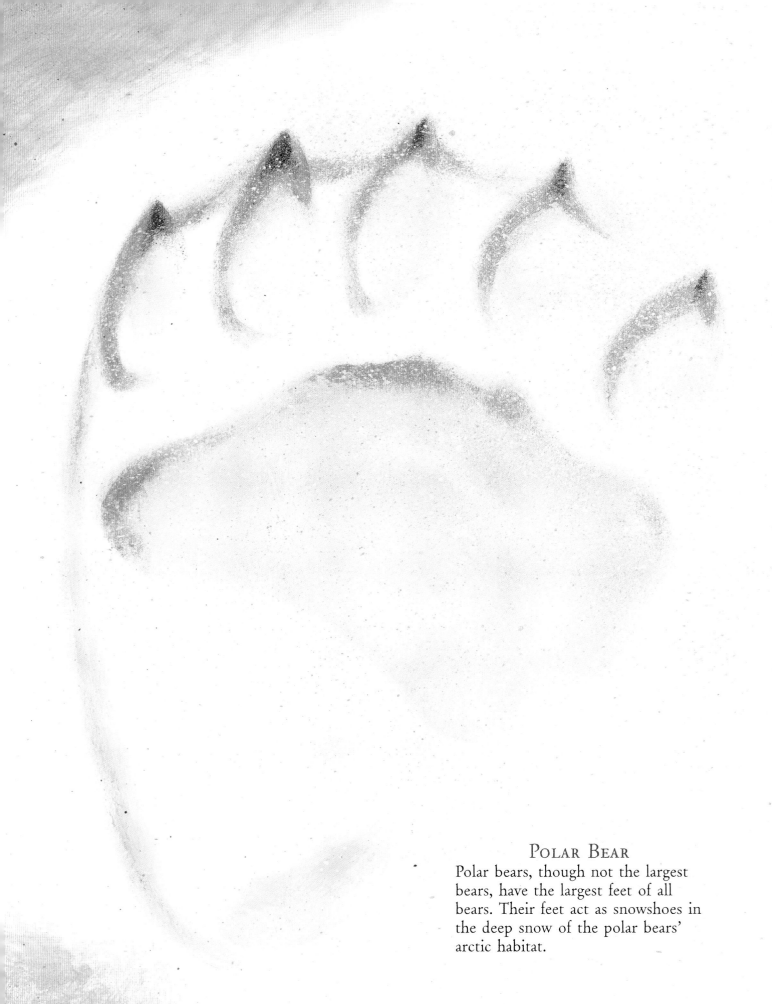

POLAR BEAR
Polar bears, though not the largest bears, have the largest feet of all bears. Their feet act as snowshoes in the deep snow of the polar bears' arctic habitat.

SNOWSHOE HARE

Small Animal Tracks

The most common animal tracks you will find will be those of small animals. Unlike larger animals, who often fill up with each meal, small animals such as raccoons, skunks, rabbits, squirrels, and mice rely on many small meals to keep them going. They must feed daily, sometimes hourly, depending on the availability of food and the absence of danger.

Small animal tracks vary as greatly as the animals that make them. Some tracks, such as those of skunks and rabbits, can be recognized by track pattern alone. All other small animal tracks are identified by shape. Note that the forefeet are usually much smaller than the hind feet.

The snowshoe hare, shown on the opposite page, lives in northern forests. It is named for its unusually large hind feet.

forefoot

hind foot

Raccoon front and hind prints

Opossum

forefoot

hind foot

forefoot

hind foot

Beaver

forefoot

hind foot

Otter

hind foot

forefoot

Muskrat

hind foot

forefoot

Armadillo

hind foot

forefoot

Porcupine

Skunk's diagonal running pattern

Mouse Pattern

tail drag

Rabbit Pattern

19

LIFE-SIZE TRACKS
OF SMALL ANIMALS

RACCOON
forefoot

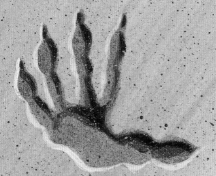

OPOSSUM
hind foot

MINK
forefoot

**LONG-TAILED
WEASEL**
forefoot

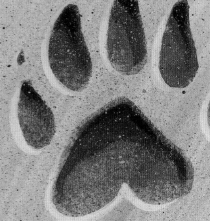

BADGER
forefoot

STRIPED SKUNK
forefoot

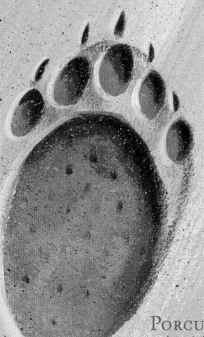

RIVER OTTER
hind foot

PORCUPINE
hind foot

RINGTAIL
forefoot

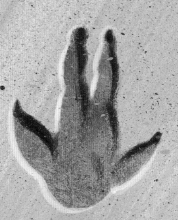

ARMADILLO
forefoot

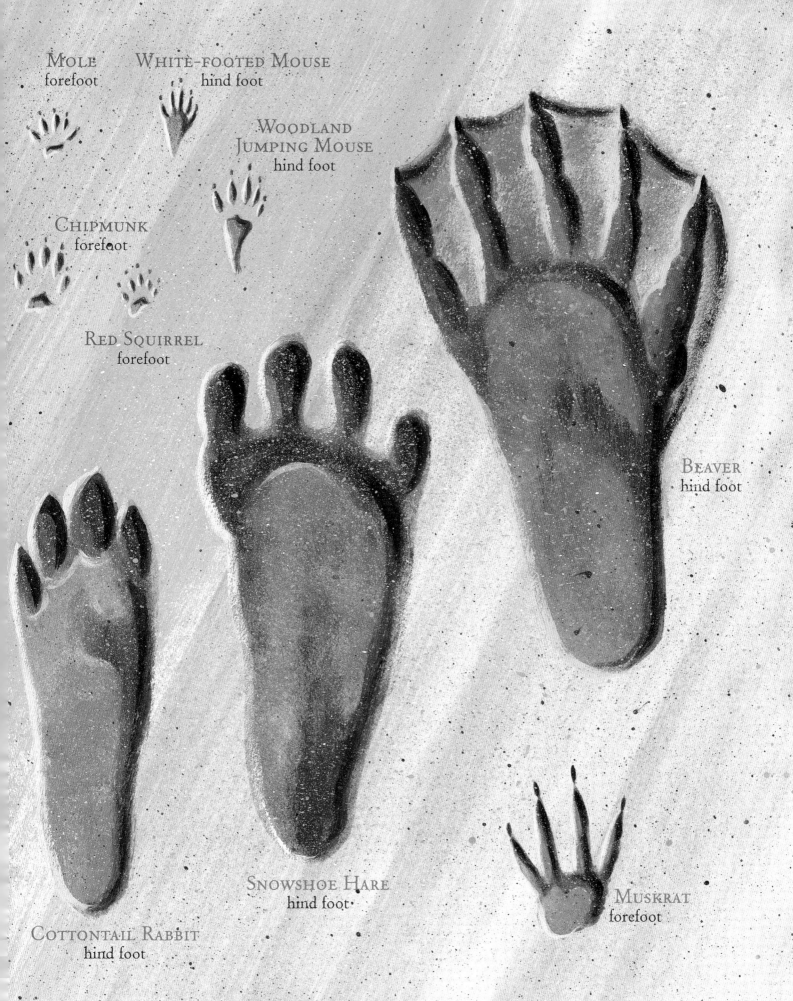

MOLE
forefoot

WHITE-FOOTED MOUSE
hind foot

WOODLAND
JUMPING MOUSE
hind foot

CHIPMUNK
forefoot

RED SQUIRREL
forefoot

BEAVER
hind foot

SNOWSHOE HARE
hind foot

COTTONTAIL RABBIT
hind foot

MUSKRAT
forefoot

21

BOBCAT

Feline Tracks

Of all the larger predators, wildcats are the most likely to use the same trails again and again. In deep snow, their habitual routes become gully trails in which feline tracks going to and coming from their hunting grounds are preserved, down out of the wind, away from blowing snow.

A cat's sharp retractable claws do not show in its tracks unless the cat has lunged to catch its prey or scratched the ground to cover its droppings. Only cats thoroughly cover their droppings.

Bobcat, lion, and jaguar paws all have three-lobed heels. The lynx, the ocelot, and the jaguarundi have single-lobed heels.

The wildcats we have in North America are, from smallest to largest: ocelot, jaguarundi, bobcat, lynx, American lion, and jaguar.

Typical cat print

Lynx

20" Domestic cat

36" Bobcat

Cat walking

Note claw marks

Cat running and lunging after prey

Tracks poked in deep snow

Bobcat foot - top Showing retractable claws

Bottom showing 3-lobed heel

25

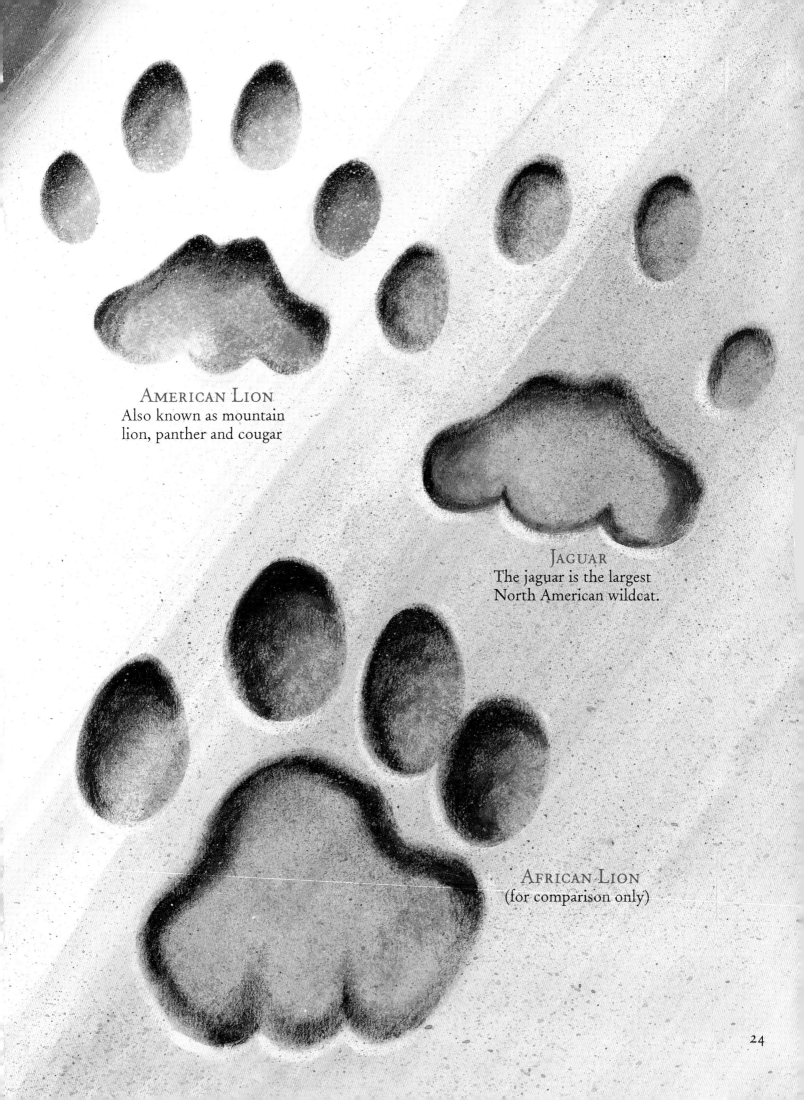

AMERICAN LION
Also known as mountain
lion, panther and cougar

JAGUAR
The jaguar is the largest
North American wildcat.

AFRICAN LION
(for comparison only)

24

LIFE-SIZE TRACKS OF FELINES

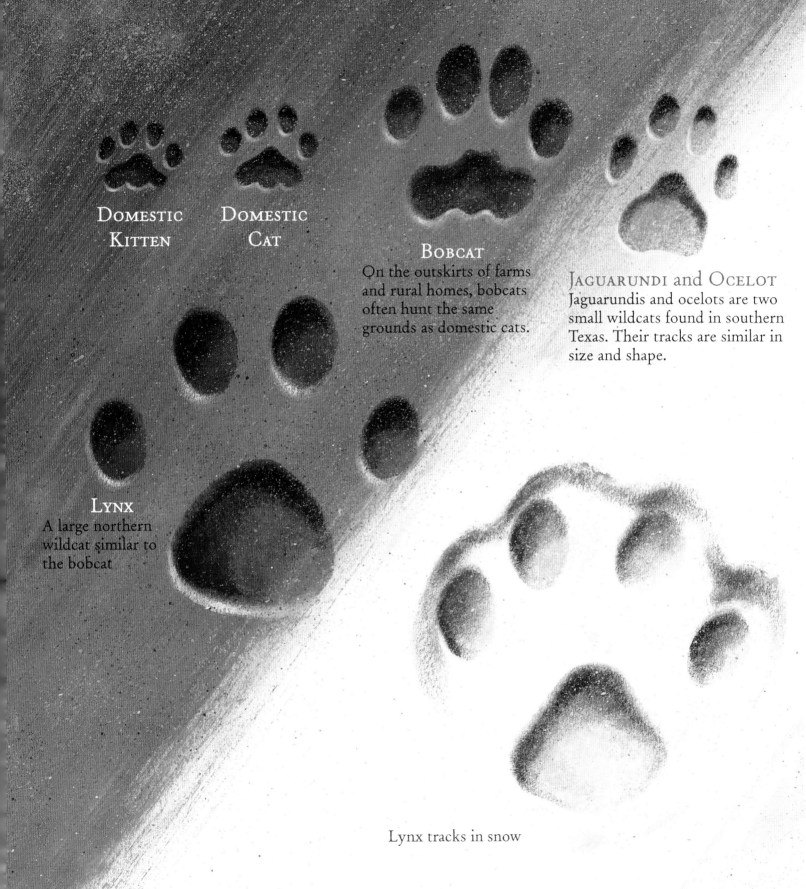

DOMESTIC KITTEN

DOMESTIC CAT

BOBCAT
On the outskirts of farms and rural homes, bobcats often hunt the same grounds as domestic cats.

JAGUARUNDI and OCELOT
Jaguarundis and ocelots are two small wildcats found in southern Texas. Their tracks are similar in size and shape.

LYNX
A large northern wildcat similar to the bobcat

Lynx tracks in snow

TIMBER WOLF

Canine Tracks

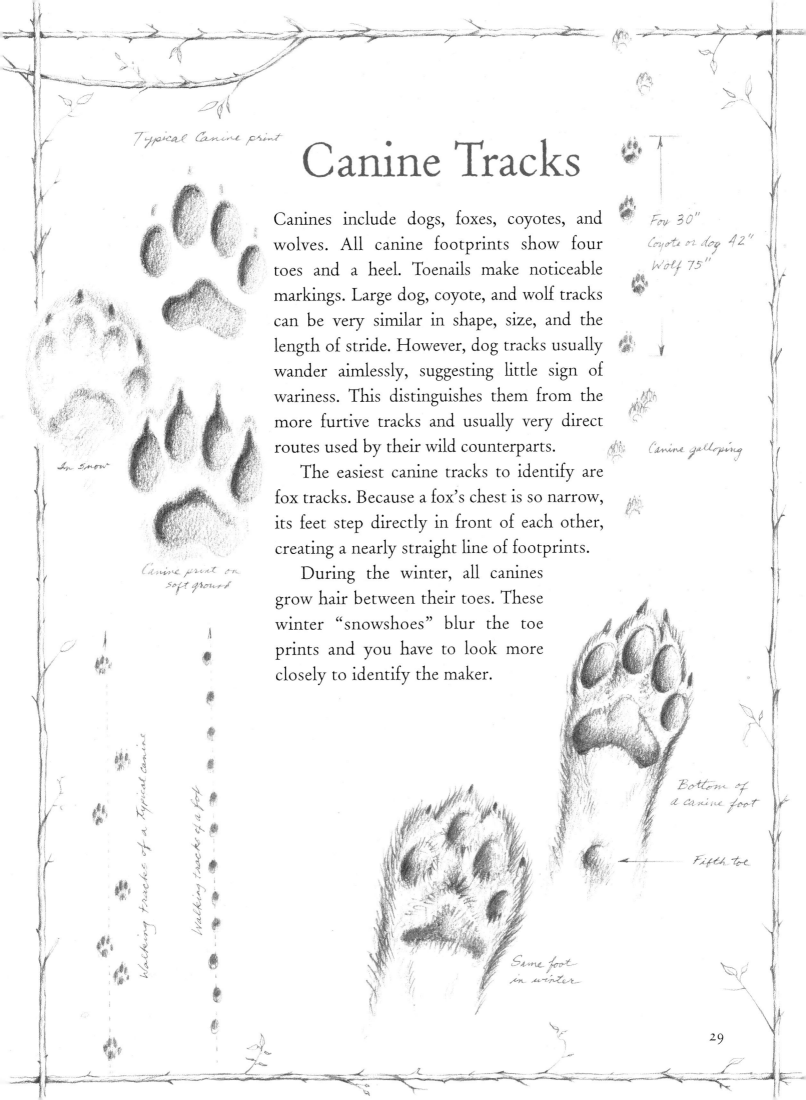

Typical Canine print

In snow

Canine print on
soft ground

Walking tracks of a Typical Canine

Walking tracks of a fox

Canines include dogs, foxes, coyotes, and wolves. All canine footprints show four toes and a heel. Toenails make noticeable markings. Large dog, coyote, and wolf tracks can be very similar in shape, size, and the length of stride. However, dog tracks usually wander aimlessly, suggesting little sign of wariness. This distinguishes them from the more furtive tracks and usually very direct routes used by their wild counterparts.

The easiest canine tracks to identify are fox tracks. Because a fox's chest is so narrow, its feet step directly in front of each other, creating a nearly straight line of footprints.

During the winter, all canines grow hair between their toes. These winter "snowshoes" blur the toe prints and you have to look more closely to identify the maker.

Fox 30"
Coyote or dog 42"
Wolf 75"

Canine galloping

Bottom of
a canine foot

Fifth toe

Same foot
in winter

29

COYOTE

ARCTIC FOX

COYOTE ON MUD

RED WOLF

TIMBER WOLF
(Also known as the gray wolf.) Wolf prints
are huge; a set of four can span 5 or 6 feet.

28

LIFE-SIZE TRACKS
OF CANINES

SMALL DOG

MEDIUM-SIZE DOG

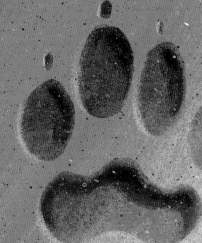

LARGE DOG

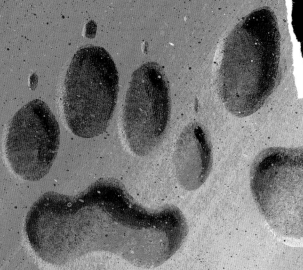

HUGE DOG

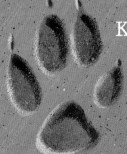

KIT FOX

RED FOX

GRAY FOX

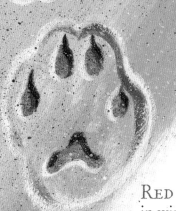

RED FOX
in winter snow

COTTONMOUTH MOCCASIN
and WHITE IBISES

Reptile & Bird Tracks

Reptile tracks often go unnoticed. Our eyes are used to looking for distinctive footprints rather than the various scrapes and marks reptiles make. But when a snake slithers across mud or a turtle drags itself over sand, a series of tracks are left that are very recognizable.

During times of drought, alligator tracks can be seen on the mud flats that were previously covered by water. Use only your binoculars to examine reptile tracks. Never follow on foot. The places where these animals go can be unsafe, and the animals can be dangerous if approached suddenly.

Bird tracks rarely travel far; then their makers take flight. Some tracks show only two footprints and then wing marks flapping away. Songbirds hop. Shorebirds and large birds such as crows and turkeys walk. All birds create the most delicate and beautiful animal tracks, evoking both earth and sky in every footprint.

The next time you go outdoors, look for wild tracks. There may be a whole story at your feet, imprinted on the mud or snow or scratched into the sand.

Snake tracks

Alligator tracks

Turtle tracks

Shell scrapes

Tail drag

Crow (a walker)

Sparrow (a hopper)

Tail drag

31

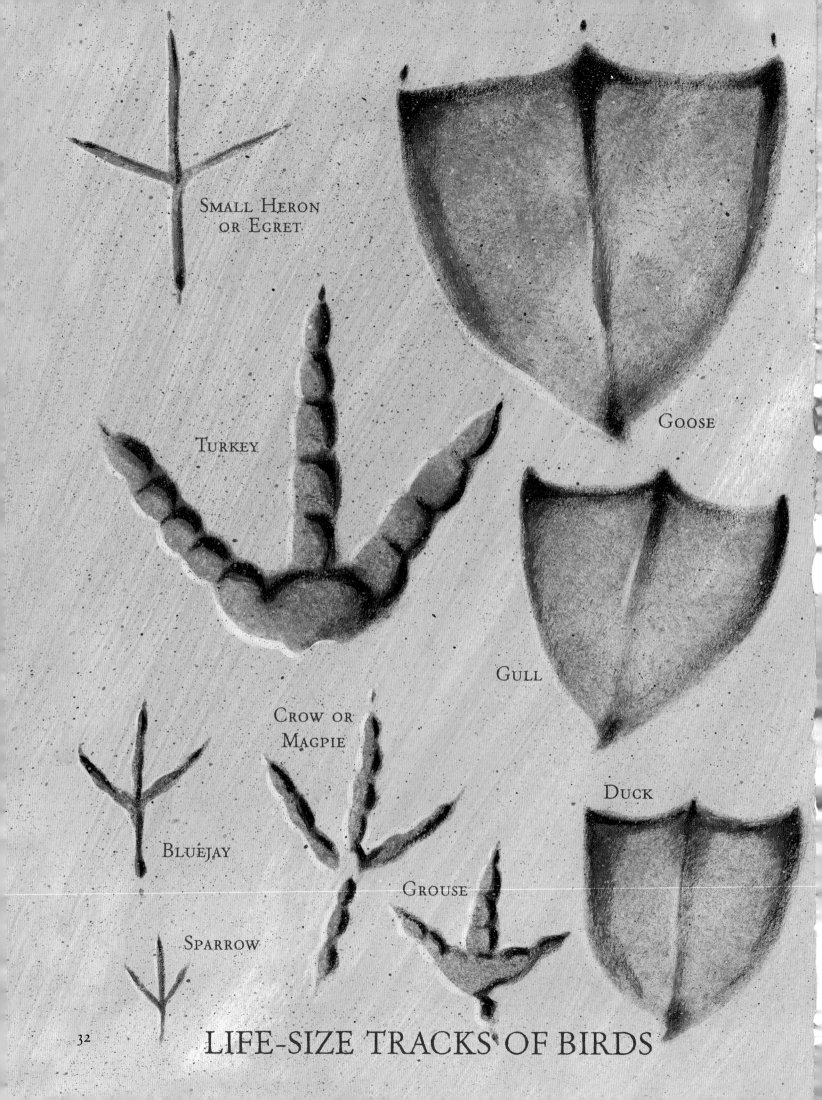

SMALL HERON
OR EGRET

GOOSE

TURKEY

GULL

CROW OR
MAGPIE

DUCK

BLUEJAY

GROUSE

SPARROW

32 LIFE-SIZE TRACKS OF BIRDS